The Faithful Durhams

The story of The Durham Light Infantry, 1758 - 1968

Text by Stephen D. Shannon
Edited by Iain Watson

DURHAM COUNTY COUNCIL
Arts, Libraries and Museums Department

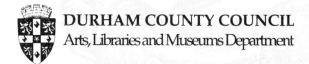

Acknowledgements: Photographs from the collections of The Durham Light Infantry Museum are the copyright of the Trustees of The Durham Light Infantry

ISBN 1-897585-02-0

The Durham Light Infantry 1758-1968

Foreword

The Durham Light Infantry Museum attracts visitors from all over the world including many former DLI soldiers and their relatives and descendants. This book has been produced by the Arts, Libraries and Museums Department of Durham County Council to tell the story of the DLI, and to provide a starting point for anyone seeking information about the Regiment and its soldiers. I hope that it will be of interest both to the general public and to the serious student of military history.

Patrick Conway, Director of Arts, Libraries and Museums, Durham County Council

The Durham Light Infantry has a proud history from the formation of the 68th Regiment of Foot in 1758 to the laying up of the Colours in the Regimental Chapel in Durham Cathedral on 12th December 1968. The DLI has very close associations with County Durham, and it was the tough fighting men of Durham who gave the regiment its reputation for absolute reliability in battle. I am delighted to see the publication of this book telling the story of the 'Faithful Durhams'.

Colonel S. J. Furness, DL, Deputy Colonel (Durham) The Light Infantry

Local Pride

While many regiments in the British Army have or have had close associations with individual counties, The Durham Light Infantry is perhaps unique in the closeness of its relationship with County Durham. The association between the Regiment and the County can be traced back to at least 1758 and continues to the present day. The DLI Museum and the Trustees and Friends of the

Laying up the old Colours, Palace Green, Durham Cathedral, 1950

DLI are all based in Durham City and the Colours of the Regiment have been laid up in the Regimental Chapel in Durham Cathedral. For many years recruiting to the Regiment was almost wholly from County Durham. Many officers who came into contact with the Regiment remarked on its particular character. Field Marshal Montgomery wrote 'It is a magnificent Regiment, steady as a rock in battle, and absolutely reliable on all occasions. The fighting men of Durham are splendid soldiers. . .'

Although Durham is a large and varied county, much of it devoted to agriculture, the image of the DLI soldier in the twentieth century is that of the

Durham miner. Lieutenant-General Sir Brian Horrocks wrote of the DLI: ' The more I saw of these tough Geordies the more I got to like and admire them. The hard life led by the miners in peacetime makes them some of the best infantry in the world.' George Butterworth who joined the DLI as a junior officer at the start of the First World War wrote that he enjoyed being with the DLI because of the calibre of the men whom he was commanding. He recorded that they were almost all strictly local, that they were almost all working men (90% of the men in his platoon being miners), and that they were NORTHERNERS ! During the First World War the DLI established a particular reputation for their abilities at trench digging - very important in this war of the trenches. The Durhams, presumably because of the skills of many former miners with pick and shovel, seemed just to disappear into the ground before the eyes of their comrades.

In August 1914, at the start of the First World War, the DLI had only nine battalions. By the end of the war, the DLI had raised forty three battalions, twenty two of which saw action overseas. These new battalions were made up of thousands of volunteers from the mines, shipyards, farms, shops, schools, offices and industries of County Durham. Many of these were given affectionate local names, like the "Durham Pals" (18th Battalion DLI), "Durham Bantams" (19th Battalion DLI) and "Wearsiders" (20th Battalion DLI). It was these men who were to forge an unbreakable link between Regiment and County and make The Durham Light Infantry a real County Regiment.

History of the DLI

Regular soldiers 1758-1881

The story of the Durham Light Infantry begins in 1758. Britain was at war with France and there was a need for more soldiers. In County Durham, General John Lambton of Lambton Castle was ordered to raise a new regiment of professional soldiers - the 68th.

Crosier Surtees, an officer of the Durham Militia, c. 1760

For the first fifty years of its life the new 68th Regiment, which at that time had few men from Durham serving in its ranks, saw little active service and fought in no major battles. The Regiment did, however, suffer casualties and, during three tours of duty in the West Indies, thousands of men died of disease. The regimental motto 'Faithful' dates from those arduous years.

In 1808, the 68th was chosen to become one of the new light infantry regiments. These regiments were intended to be a fast-moving strike force. The soldiers were given extensive training and equipped with lighter muskets and new clothing. The soldiers now took their orders from the call of the bugle and not from the beat of the drum. From that time the Regiment adopted the bugle as its badge. In 1811 the new 68th Light Infantry was sent to Portugal to join the fight against Napoleon. As part of the Duke of Wellington's army, the 68th Light Infantry took part in the great battles of Salamanca, Vittoria, Pyrenees, Nivelle and Orthes, as well as in numerous skirmishes with the French that proved the value of the new light infantry training. In these battles the Regiment won its first battle honours.

In 1814, with the Peninsular War over and the French driven out of Spain, the 68th Light Infantry was sent to Ireland to rebuild its strength. The Regiment did not take part in the campaign that led to Napoleon's final defeat at Waterloo and the 68th Light Infantry was not to see active service again until it set sail for the Crimea in 1854.

During those long years of peace, the Regiment served in garrisons in Ireland, Gibraltar, Malta, Canada and the West Indies, with only three years in England. Discipline and training in the Regiment were allowed to slip until, in 1842, command was given to Lord William Paulet. He transformed the Regiment, improving the standards of every officer and man, until, in 1848, an inspecting general described the 68th as a 'beautiful regiment'. Lord Paulet later became Colonel of the Regiment (1864-93). In 1893 he was paid a remarkable tribute when the whole of the 1st Battalion attended his funeral.

Soldiers of the 68th Light Infantry, Crimean War, 1855

Between 1854 and 1856, the 68th Light Infantry fought in the Crimean War, taking part in the battles of Alma, Balaclava, Inkerman and the siege of Sebastopol. At Inkerman, on 5th November 1854, the Regiment fought off repeated attacks by a Russian force many times its size. During the battle, the 68th were the only British troops to fight in red, having thrown off their grey greatcoats to reach their ammunition pouches. Casualties were heavy but, once again, more soldiers died of disease in the Crimea than in battle. Two soldiers of the 68th who had distinguished themselves in battle - John Byrne and Thomas de Courcey Hamilton - were awarded the newly created Victoria Cross.

Many of the Crimean veterans were to see action again in New Zealand when, in 1864, the 68th Light Infantry was sent to assist the European

Band and Colours, 106th Bombay Light Infantry, India, c. 1869

colonists in their war with the Maoris. At Gate Pah in April 1864 the Regiment took part in an unsuccessful attack on a Maori fort. Two months later, the Maoris were defeated at Te Ranga, where John Murray won the Regiment's third Victoria Cross. This was the last action in which the 68th Light Infantry fought. In 1866 the Regiment left New Zealand and returned to garrison duty. In 1881 it became the 1st Battalion DLI.

The second of the regiments which were, in 1881, to become The Durham Light Infantry was formed, as the 2nd Bombay European Infantry, in India in 1839. It was not part of the British Army but part of the East India Company which effectively ruled India. There was no connection with Durham at this time and the Regiment recruited men from all over Britain and Ireland. The Regiment was reorganised as light infantry in 1840 and in 1856 took part in the invasion of Persia (Iran), winning its only battle honours. When the Regiment returned to India the country was in the grip of mutiny. After peace was restored in 1858, the India Act was passed ending the rule of the East India Company and transferring the Company's soldiers to the British Army. The 2nd Bombay became the 106th Light Infantry and then, in 1881, the 2nd Battalion DLI.

Militia and Volunteers

When the DLI was formed in 1881 it included not only the regular soldiers who made up the 1st and 2nd Battalions but also the Militia and Volunteers of County Durham. The Militia was organised by counties, with the local gentry acting as officers and the soldiers selected by ballot. It was intended for home defence only and, in time of war, the Militia

Sergeants and their families, 2nd North Durham Militia, Gilesgate, Durham, c.1874

garrisoned towns and coastal forts, releasing regular soldiers for service overseas. The Durham Militia was formed in 1759 at Barnard Castle by the Earl of Darlington. During the Napoleonic Wars, the Durham Militia spent over twenty years on garrison duty from Portsmouth to Glasgow. After the war, it fell into decay but was revived in 1853 and divided into the 1st South Durham Militia at Barnard Castle and the 2nd North Durham Militia at Durham City. In 1881, these Militia units became the 3rd and 4th Battalions of the newly formed DLI but continued to meet only once a year for training. In the Boer War, 1899-1902, these battalions went on active service overseas for the first and last time. During the First World War, they did garrison duty on the Durham coast but, in 1920, were put into 'suspended animation'. They took no part in the Second World War and were finally disbanded in 1953.

The first Volunteers of County Durham were amateur soldiers who formed local defence units in the County during the Napoleonic Wars. These

Volunteers, who bought all their own uniforms and equipment, saw no action and were all disbanded by 1815. In 1859, fear of France led to a revival of the Volunteers. In County Durham, these new Volunteers were organised as rifle clubs with members paying a subscription. Nineteen Rifle Volunteer units were formed in Durham. These part-time soldiers were formed into Volunteer battalions of the DLI in 1881. In 1908 they were renamed Territorials and they played a major role in the First and Second World Wars.

Durham Light Infantry 1881 - 1968

In 1885, the 2nd Battalion was the first element of the newly formed DLI to go into action, when they formed part of an army sent to defend Egypt. The invasion from the Sudan was halted at Ginnis, the last battle fought by the British Army in red rather than the new khaki tunics.

The Boer War in South Africa, 1899-1902, saw all

Watching for the Boers, 3rd Battalion DLI, South Africa, 1901

parts of The Durham Light Infantry in action together for the first time. The 1st Battalion took part in the relief of Ladysmith, fighting at Colenso, Spion Kop and at Vaal Krantz, where the soldiers distinguished themselves in a fierce uphill attack against the Boers. Later the 2nd Battalion sent a Mounted Infantry Unit from India, whilst the 3rd and 4th Battalions, plus Volunteers from Durham, also saw action.

Trench warfare and new weapons led to huge

Off to the Western Front, 17th Battalion DLI, Barnard Castle, 1915

numbers of casualties in the First World War. In September 1914 the 2nd Battalion lost as many men in one day as the entire Regiment had lost in the Boer War. In Spring 1915, the Territorials, fighting at Ypres, lost a third of their strength in just a few weeks. The Battle of the Somme in 1916 was, for the new battalions of volunteers, a baptism of fire. On 1st July the "Durham Pals" (18th Battalion DLI) lost over half their strength killed or wounded.

Scenes from our Daily Life.

SCENES FROM OUR DAILY LIFE. No. 2—Trench Mortar Strafe.

Adam Wakenshaw VC

The Durham Light Infantry fought in every major battle of the Great War - at Ypres, Arras, Messines, Cambrai, on the Somme and in the mud of Passchendaele. The Regiment was awarded six Victoria Crosses but the cost to the Regiment and County was horrific with nearly 13,000 men dead and thousands more gassed, wounded or taken prisoner.

After the First World War, the DLI was reduced to two Regular and five Territorial battalions. The Regular battalions, which served in the 1920s and 1930s in India, China, Egypt and at home, had few problems with recruitment as a result of the high level of unemployment in County Durham.

During the Second World War, 1939-45, the army needed specialist units rather than infantry and the DLI raised far fewer new battalions. The eight battalions which saw active service, however, fought with distinction in every major theatre of the War - at Dunkirk, in North Africa, Malta, Sicily, Italy, Burma and, in Europe, from D-Day to the final defeat of Nazi Germany.

Two Victoria Crosses were won by DLI soldiers during the Second World War. The first Army Victoria Cross of the war was awarded to Richard Annand of the 2nd Battalion. In May 1940 he drove off an attack on a bridge on the River Dyle in Belgium by throwing grenades onto the German soldiers below. Afterwards, though badly wounded himself, he rescued a wounded soldier. In June 1942, at Mersa

The Wakenshaw Gun

Matruh in North Africa, the eleventh and last DLI Victoria Cross was awarded posthumously to Adam Wakenshaw of the 9th Battalion DLI, who continued to man his anti-tank gun though mortally wounded.

Casualties during the Second World War were far lower than in the First World War but in several fierce actions, at Arras, Mareth, Primosole Bridge and Kohima, for example, the Regiment suffered heavy losses.

After the Second World War, the DLI was, once again, reduced in size until only the 1st Battalion remained. The 2nd Battalion was disbanded in 1948, re-raised in 1952, only to be finally disbanded in 1954. As for the Territorials, the 9th Battalion became part of the Parachute Regiment

Stretcher bearers at Kohima, 2nd Battalion DLI, India, 1944

in 1948 and in 1967 the 6th and 8th Battalions were amalgamated for a short time before being disbanded. Thus, after 1945, only the 1st Battalion saw action overseas. The 1st Battalion DLI fought as part of the United Nations forces in Korea in 1952-53. Conditions were almost like those of the trenches during the Great War. This Battalion later served in Cyprus and was stationed in Berlin in 1961 - the time when the Berlin Wall was built. The last campaign fought by the DLI was in 1966 in the jungles and mountains of Borneo. In 1968, whilst the battalion was serving in Cyprus with the United Nations, it was announced that The Durham Light Infantry would become part of the new Light

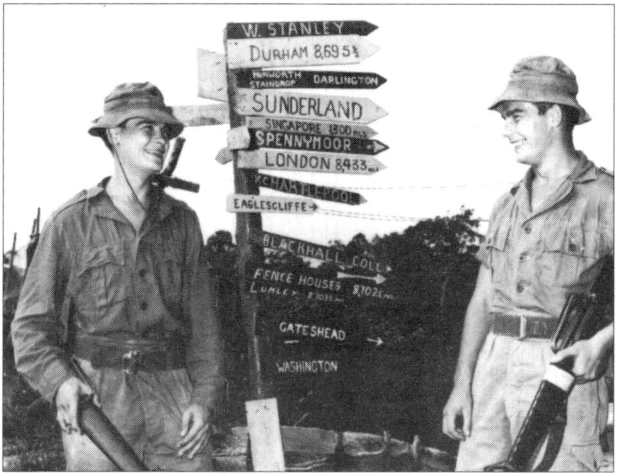

The last campaign, 1st Battalion DLI, Borneo, 1966

Infantry and the Regiment would lose its county name.

In Durham Cathedral, on 12th December 1968, The Durham Light Infantry paraded its Colours for the last time. After two hundred years of history, County Durham's own Regiment was no more.

Experiences of War

Personal accounts written by DLI soldiers in action

Peninsular War -Private John Green served with the 68th Light Infantry in the battle against Napoleon's forces in Spain. He published his reminiscences in 1827. This extract describes what happened after he was wounded at St Sebastian in August 1813

The enemy having obtained a strong reinforcement, now advanced in close column, their drums beating in order to keep them together. We again retreated, and I narrowly escaped being taken prisoner; for I was almost exhausted with running. As we retreated, we kept up a steady and well-directed fire, and gained the summit of the hill in good order, not having a single man taken prisoner . . . I had only fired one shot, when a ball struck me, entering my left side, a little below my heart. At first, I felt nothing; in about ten seconds, however, I fell to the ground, turned sick and faint, and expected every moment to expire having an intolerable burning pain in my left side . . . Mr Reid, our regimental surgeon, came to me, and ran his little finger into my side, to clear it of any substance that might be lodged in the wound. I cried aloud by reason of the pain it occasioned. "Silence!" said the surgeon, "it is for your good." The ball could not be extracted. A little dry lint was put over the wound, and a bandage bound tight round my body: my clothes were put on, and I was laid on the ground, but was so full of pain, that I could not rest more than two minutes in any one posture . . . In the afternoon, an old soldier, who had been used to the hospitals, came round and dressed our wounds: the old man did very well, for after he had dressed my wound I seemed easier. We sent a man to headquarters, to draw provisions, and procure medical assistance: he returned on the 3rd September with our bread and meat, but had drunk and sold the rum: had he been with the regiment, he would have paid dear for his base conduct. A surgeon arrived with thirty mules to carry us to the general hospital: he dressed our wounds, and then gave orders for us to march at two o'clock in the afternoon. This being the fourth day since we had been wounded, our wounds were very sore: some were crying by reason of excessive pain in their fractured limbs. As for myself; I wept like a child. We were the worst off in descending the mountains: the mules slided down for three or four yards together; and how I got to the end of my journey I can scarcely tell . . . Our sufferings while descending these lofty hills were indescribable: I really never expected to reach the bottom alive; it was like cutting my body to pieces. I cried, screamed, prayed and wished to die: my companions were in the same way; some were praying, others weeping and moaning; and we presented a scene of the completest misery and wretchedness. We at length arrived at the bottom of the mountains, and were quartered at General Graham's headquarters, where we had again to lie on the bare floor without a covering. Here we heard of the fall of St. Sebastian: it was taken by storm on the 31st of August, the very day on which I was wounded, after a severe conflict . . . After remaining a short time in the hospital, I was put into a ward, consisting of fifteen wounded men belonging to different regiments: nothing could exceed the miserable appearance of the patients, for some of us were almost lost with vermin, not having been able to clean ourselves for several days. Every man had a kind of bed made of two biscuit-bags sewed together, and filled with fern, or what we call brackens, which was very comfortable in comparison with what we had been accustomed to. On the 8th of September the hospital stores arrived from England, and we were served out with everything that could conduce to our comfort and health. Each man was provided with a harden bed-tick filled with straw, two blankets, one pair of sheets and one mug: this happy change caused us partly to forget our late misfortunes.

John Green, Vicissitudes of a Soldier's Life

Crimean War - Colour Sergeant William Henry Foster, serving with the 68th Light Infantry, wrote the following letter home from a camp near Sebastopol in the Crimea.

10th January 1856

Dear Mother,

I hope you won't be uneasy at my not answering your kind letter sooner as I have had some severe duty on hand lately. I am very happy to be able to tell you we are (that is the army) in excellent health and spirits; plenty of food and clothing and Huts to live in but the weather is so changeable from cold to heat, frost to mud that some few of us have severe colds - it's nothing to see the Heights covered with snow at night and the next morning no sign of it appears, and perhaps the next day we are up to our ankles in mud - such is our climate. Dear Mother, we see nothing of the enemy except when we go on Guard in Sebastopol. The last time I went there I ventured to the ruins of the famous Fort Paul, and under cover of large stones I could see them load and fire their guns quite plain, they being on one side of the harbour and us on the other. They send shells very near us but do no harm, in fact I am so used to them that I stand up quite unconcerned when they burst about 50 yards from one and strangers, that visit Sebastopol run about in all directions when they hear a shell whistling through the air and very much frightened, such is the case with everyone not used to be under fire.

Boer War - The following two extracts are from letters home written by 1st Battalion DLI soldiers serving in South Africa during the Boer War. Both were written in

February 1900 after the attack on Vaal Krantz.

. . . You should have seen the gallant Durham Light Infantry take the hill. It was a fine piece of work, taking it at the point of the bayonet. When the other regiments, who were watching at the other side of the Tugela River saw that the faithful Durhams had taken the hill they sent up a ringing cheer. We had two officers killed and five wounded. I saw many Boers lying about the hill. One had an arm and a leg off . One Boer got two bayonets put through him. You should have seen the 'sods' run when they heard our war cry. We yell, and no mistake when we do charge. I pity the Boers if we get them on the open plain. They lie shooting from behind the rocks till we get up to them, and then they throw up their heads and ask for mercy, and if you are not careful they would pick up their rifles and shoot you down. I would give them mercy if I had my own way with a rifle bullet.

Private. R. Newton

... I got out of our last engagement safe and sound. It took place on the 5th and 6th of this month at Vaal Krantz. We have had rather a rough time of it this last month. Since leaving Frere Camp we have been without blankets and tents. Corned beef and biscuits have been our share of high living, with a tin of jam thrown in now and again. A fair amount of rain made but little difference: we lay down and slept through it all. We have had some very long marches, the heat being terrible. . . As soon as daybreak arrived the Boers opened fire on our position with shells and bullets and one of their dear little guns which Tommy calls the "buck-up-gun". It fired six shells in quick succession and made it rather uncomfortable for us. It caused more damage amongst us than all their other firing, and we were not under rocks or stones, but simply behind a little entrenchment. We were told to keep well under cover, and some food arrived at the bottom of the hill soon after. We had been looking anxiously for it, but it was very risky to leave to go and

fetch any as if anyone showed his head a volley was fired at him, so some thought the best part of valour was to stop where they were and wait.

Private. L. S. Woolley

World War 1

This letter was written in 1916 by Private Harry Lockey, 20th Battalion DLI, from a hospital in Cambridge. He was never to recover from the wounds he received, and he died in 1921.

One chap was mortally wounded, and asked to be taken away. It was like hailstone-storm with shells, but I picked him up and managed to get him carried to our lines and was lowering him into the trench when a shell burst behind and hit me in the back.; it knocked me into the air, and fell back into No Man's Land again. With the concussion of the shell I lost the use of my legs. I tried hard to get away. I knew more shells would drop there, but I could not. Well I had not laid long till another did drop and buried my legs with lumps of soil. I was there about an hour before I was got out. More than I expected, to be alive. I lay in the trench 3 hours before the stretchers came and our Major stayed with me all the time. The poor chap died that I carried out, he was in an awful mess. Well Old Fritz got one onto us that time, but we are not down-hearted yet. I think there would be about 70 of us wounded and killed together out of about 150. It was not long before I got the use of my legs. I think I was very lucky, and have nothing to grumble about. I am sorry it is so far away, but I will have to hurry up and get better and come and see you all. It is a treat being here. it is a big change from FRANCE.

The following extract comes from an account of the Battle at Hooge, Belgium, written in 1915 by Sergeant Isaac Plews, 2nd Battalion DLI. It describes the chaos and confusion that characterised many of the actions of the Great War.

Morning of the 10th had a rum issue at 12.30 am and moved out of the wood at 1.45 and laid out at the edge of the second line to advance. We were the attacking Regiment. At 2.45 am our Artillery opened fire, started by a 9.2 and it was a most glorious sight to see. At 3.05 am our guns lifted the range and we started the advance under a very feeble rifle fire and little shell fire, but it increased as we got nearer to enemy's lines. A general mix up followed of all our Battalion and we advanced too far. We were under our own Artillery fire and we dug ourselves in between the enemy's 2nd and 3rd lines, about 6 yards off their 3rd line. It was hell just at that time but we very gamely stuck to it. All our Company officers were either killed or wounded only Mr Sheriff was left and a very brave man he is too.

Sergeant Robert Constantine of the 9th Battalion DLI wrote a remarkable series of letters home which were preserved by his family. He was killed in action on 15th September 1916 during the Battle of the Somme:

24 September 1915

The grub we have had up to now is cruel, noot but hard biscuits, I have a bit bread, but I had to buy it, it is different bread to what you get in England. I suppose I'll have to do without luxuries now as money is gone. We are expecting to be in the fighting line in a few days time and I'll write again shortly and let you know what it is like.

6 August 1916

We are in amongst some Australian sappers just now and what a carry on they make with the Geordies, as they call us. They think we are the hardest lot they have ever come across and sure we have some hard cases in our crush - don't care for anything.

World War II

While most of Britain's attention in 1944 was concentrated on the war in Europe, the 2nd Battalion DLI were engaged in fighting a bloody war in Burma against the Japanese.

*I stood up and smack I was knocked round and found my arm hanging limp and useless and numb. I believe I said '**** it, hit again'. I thought it was broken but it didn't hurt which was fortunate. I crawled round with it hanging for a bit and then got a rifle sling and hung it in that round my neck. After that I couldn't do much except with my left hand. We were lining the backs of trench-roofs and keeping our eyes skinned . . . I can't remember daylight coming. I remember talking to Roger Stock and hearing 5 minutes later that he was dead. But the night was nearly over thank God. We could see Kuki Picquet and they too could see us. The LMG' s opened up and we were in the open on a forward slope. We couldn't spot them. I went forward with a Bren gunner to try but he got us first and the gunner had his hair parted by a burst. All he said was "My God, I've got a bloody headache" ! We shifted and I found a good billet behind a dead Jap. Not a bad little chap - but he stared at me. Anyway he was useful. I never thought of looking in his pockets for papers or loot, it only struck me afterwards. He kept me company for some time. 'A' company were preparing for a counter attack and Peter Stockton came up and had a* *chat to find out what the situation was. They went in in fine style. Peter leading with his Kukri. They got in to the trenches and fought their way along a bit but the Japs were too strong. Peter was killed almost immediately. The wounded started straggling back and the b - s opened up on them with their LMG's. The stretcher bearers were beyond all praise and I've never seen such superb and inspiring courage. They knelt in the open and patched the chaps up and carried them back and came back for more. They were unstintingly and without thought for themselves. Col: Spencer and Ward were put in for the V.C. They got NOTHING - not even a mention from Delhi.*

Major Pat Rome, Kohima, Burma, 1944

Major George Wood of the 6th Battalion DLI recorded his "Thoughts and Impressions prior to Battle" before embarking for the D-Day Landings:

My thoughts are very mixed - What a grand set of men - Hope we don't lose too many of the old faces this time - Already they've seen so much and done so much - They know what it's all about, what to expect, they've done it before - No false illusions - War is not a pleasant pastime, besides we cannot possibly hope for such an easy landing as we had in Sicily. The English Countryside is at its best - So lovely - How long will it be, before we see it again - I believe this thought is in everyone's mind - I wonder what my wife is doing at this moment - It's such a nice day, I expect she is taking Baby for a walk. Lord, how heavy and irksome all this equipment feels - Christmas tree order the troops call it - However we can't do without any of it - It's all essential. I suppose we will sail tonight - I have never been sea-sick before- Hope we have a smooth crossing.

Major George Wood, 5th June 1944

The DLI Museum and Displays

The Durham Light Infantry Museum is dedicated to the history of The Durham Light Infantry and the units from which it was formed: the 68th and 106th Light Infantry, the Durham Militia and the many Volunteer Corps which were raised throughout the County at times of national emergency.

"Is it real?" - school children (plus grandfather) during a class visit to the DLI Museum

The Museum collects, conserves, records and displays material relevant to the history of these units. The displays tell the story of these units and the men who served in them across two hundred years of history, in the armies of great soldiers such as the Duke of Wellington and Field Marshal Montgomery. Museum staff organise educational activities for schools as well as regular lectures on military topics. Other events held at the Museum include military vehicle rallies and band concerts.

The Museum is owned and managed by Durham County Council through the Arts, Libraries and Museums Department, while the collections

Fur Cap, Durham Militia, c. 1760

belong to the Trustees of The Durham Light Infantry.

Displays on the ground floor of the Museum chronicle the history of the DLI up to the outbreak of the Great War. The first section concerns the Durham Militia and Durham Volunteers. Objects on show include a very rare fur cap worn by a Militia officer about 1760, an extremely fine engraved wine glass from the Chester le Street Volunteers and the Colours of both the Teesdale and South Shields Volunteers. The story of the 68th Regiment follows, with displays on the Peninsular, Crimean and New Zealand Wars. The size of the tunics worn at that time shows that some of the soldiers must have been comparatively small and thin. Many of them may not only have been very young but also poorly nourished. In the New Zealand display are several fine watercolours painted by Horatio Robley, an officer of the 68th. After a display of items from the 106th Light Infantry, including the centrepiece of the Colour carried into battle in Persia in 1856, the story of the DLI is traced from 1881 to 1914, with displays on Egypt and the Boer War. The khaki uniforms shown in these cases were relatively new at the time having been developed for fighting in India. The tin of chocolate sent in 1900 by Queen Victoria to her soldiers in South Africa still contains the chocolate!

The story of the Regiment from 1914 to 1968 is told on the Lower Ground Floor. Scenes from the First World War depict a dug-out and trenches, with models dressed in original uniforms, including a tunic worn by Roland Bradford who won the Victoria Cross in 1916. These scenes, however, cannot convey the full horror of the Western Front.

The Second World War displays feature the battle dress worn by Richard Annand when he won the

The Durham Light Infantry Medal Room

Victoria Cross in 1940 and the actual anti-tank gun on which Adam Wakenshaw VC fought and died in 1942. The Lower Ground Floor displays conclude with the Korean War and the campaign in Borneo.

The Medal Room, opened by Princess Alexandra in 1988, is acknowledged as the finest Medal Room to be seen in any regimental museum. Seven original Victoria Crosses are on display, including those of Roland Bradford, at 26 the youngest British General during the First World War, and Adam Wakenshaw, the last Durham Light Infantryman to gain the Victoria Cross. Over 1200 medals are on show, representing over 300 men who served in The Durham Light Infantry. Displays are arranged by campaign with a central display of exceptionally fine groups of medals. Detailed labels, plus over 100 photographs, allow visitors to read the full, fascinating stories of the men behind the medals - the men who made The Durham Light Infantry.

Finding out more about the DLI

Want to find out more? Perhaps a relative or friend served with the DLI? Maybe you're just inquisitive about the fighting men of County Durham's own regiment? If you want information about the DLI and the soldiers who served in it, the DLI Museum is the best place to start. There are many ways in which the Museum can help. For example, the Museum has produced guides to its records for the First and Second World Wars, which include extensive bibliographies.

Pre-World War 1

The Museum has a set of Medal Rolls that list the names and, most importantly, the regimental numbers of all who fought in, for example, the Crimean War or the Boer War. With this information you can write to the Public Record Office, Kew, Richmond, Surrey to get access to the actual service records of these men.

World War 1, 1914-1918

Some soldier's records are held at the Army Record Office, Bourne Avenue, Hayes, Middlesex, but many records were destroyed in 1940. The Army Record Office will only be able to help if you already have the soldier's name, rank, number and regiment.

For DLI soldiers who were killed in action or died of wounds during World War I the Museum can tell you number, rank, battalion and date of death. Other records in the Museum, for example war diaries and battalion histories, will give the circumstances of the soldier's death. If you want to know where the soldier is buried or commemorated, you should contact the Commonwealth War Graves Commission, 2 Marlow Road, Maidenhead, Berskshire.

The Museum also has records, including maps, relating to the award of gallantry medals (for example, the Military Medal). These records may provide considerable detail on the acts which led to the medal being awarded. Another useful source for the First World War are local newspapers, which, before 1917, printed obituaries, medal awards, letters from the Western Front and even photographs of local men. Various local newspapers for the period may be consulted at Durham City and Darlington branch libraries.

World War 2 and after (1939-1968)

Soldiers' records for these years will be found at the Army Record Office at Hayes. These records are confidential and will only be released on the written authority of the soldier concerned or his next of kin. For details of a soldier's medals, you should write to the Army Medal Office, 2 Worcester Road, Droitwich, Worcs.

The DLI Museum has some records and battalion histories for the Second World War. These are particularly useful for tracing casualties and gallantry awards.

Glossary

Artillery general name for all cannon and heavy guns.

Battalion part of a regiment. A battalion usually fought as a unit led by a lieutenant colonel. During the First World War, a battalion contained about 1000 men.

Battle Honours names of battles or campaigns in which a regiment took part. A regiment's Battle Honours were sewn on its colours.

Bren Gun light machine gun used by the British Army during the Second World War.

Colours flags carried by an infantry regiment. Each regiment had two flags, a Regimental Colour and a King's or Queen's Colour.

Company part of a battalion, led by a captain. During the First World War, there were four companies in a battalion, each about 250 men strong.

Kukri heavy curved knife used by Gurkha (Indian) soldiers.

LMG light machine gun.

Militia home defence force in which the soldiers were selected for service by ballot.

Musket infantry soldier's smooth-barrelled firearm, (later replaced by the rifle.)

Regiment	historic unit of the British Army, often named after the county where it recruited its soldiers. A regiment was divided into battalions.
Sapper	soldier involved in engineering works.
Territorial	part-time volunteer soldier.